D1117058

Monkeys

Pebble Plus

Pygmy Marmosets

by Mary R. Dunn

Consulting Editor: Gail Saunders-Smith, PhD

Consultant: Lori Perkins,
Vice President of Collections
Zoo Atlanta, Atlanta, Georgia

CAPSTONE PRESS
a capstone imprint

Pebble Plus is published by Capstone Press,
1710 Roe Crest Drive, North Mankato, Minnesota 56003
www.capstonepub.com

Library of Congress Cataloging-in-Publication Data
Dunn, Mary R.
Pygmy marmosets / by Mary Dunn.
p. cm.—(Pebble plus. Monkeys)
Includes bibliographical references and index.
Summary: "Full-color photographs and simple text introduce pygmy marmosets"—Provided by publisher.
ISBN 978-1-62065-107-0 (library binding)
ISBN 978-1-4765-1081-1 (eBook PDF)
1. Pygmy marmoset—Juvenile literature. I. Title.
QL737.P925D856 2013
599.8'4—dc23   2012024131

Editorial Credits
Jeni Wittrock, editor; Bobbie Nuytten, designer; Svetlana Zhurkin, media researcher; Eric Manske, production specialist

Photo Credits
Alamy: Barry Turner, 13; Dreamstime: Lukas Blazek, 7, 15; Getty Images: Gregory MD, 17; Minden Pictures: Claus Meyer, cover, 19, Konrad Wothe, 21; Nature Picture Library: David Kjaer, 5; Newscom: Danita Delimont Photography/Pete Oxford, 9; Shutterstock: Eric Gevaert, 1, Michael Lynch, 11

Note to Parents and Teachers

The Monkeys set supports national science standards related to life science. This book describes and illustrates pygmy marmoset monkeys. The images support early readers in understanding the text. The repetition of words and phrases helps early readers learn new words. This book also introduces early readers to subject-specific vocabulary words, which are defined in the Glossary section. Early readers may need assistance to read some words and to use the Table of Contents, Glossary, Read More, Internet Sites, and Index sections of the book.

Printed in the United States of America in North Mankato, Minnesota.
092012   006933CGS13

Table of Contents

Mini Monkeys

Pygmy marmosets are the world's smallest monkeys. These soft, brownish-gray monkeys are the size of chipmunks.

Pygmy marmosets

make their homes

near the Amazon River.

These mammals hide in

thick South American forests.

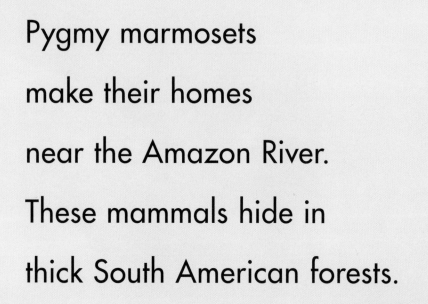

where pygmy marmosets live

Tails, Claws, and Teeth

Pygmy marmosets' tails are longer than their bodies. Long tails help the pygmies balance while darting from tree to tree.

6 feet
(183 cm)

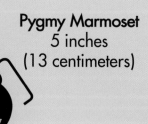

Pygmy Marmoset
5 inches
(13 centimeters)

Unlike most monkeys,
pygmy marmosets have
pointed claws. Sharp claws
and teeth help them dig
for food in the trees.

Finding Food

Pygmy marmosets chew holes in tree bark to lick sap from the trees. They also chomp on insects. Sometimes they snack on fruit.

13

Growing Up

Female pygmy marmosets usually have twins about every six months. Newborns are about as big as a human's thumb.

Pygmy marmosets care
for their babies. They carry
newborns on their backs.
In the wild, pygmy marmosets
live about 12 years.

Staying Safe

Pygmy marmosets watch out for each other. They travel in troops of two to six monkeys. Their coat colors help them hide in the forest.

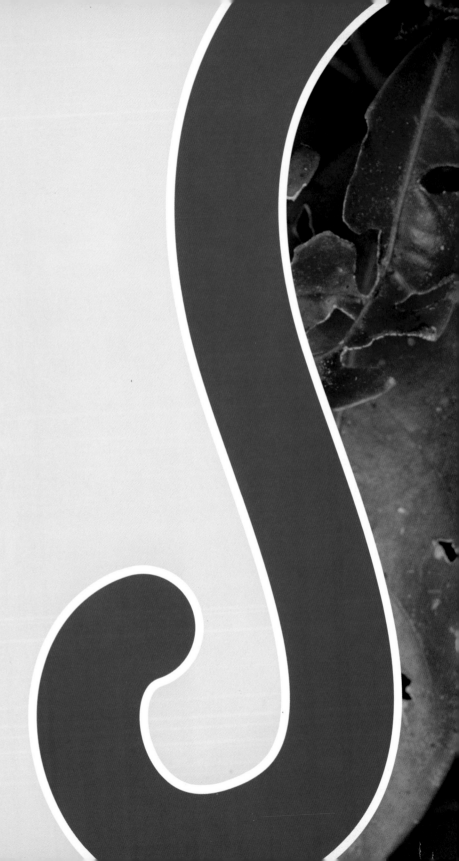

Pygmy marmosets' predators
are eagles, hawks, snakes,
and cats. But pygmies are fast
and hard to catch. Pygmies stick
together to stay safe.

Glossary

balance—to keep steady and not fall over

chomp—to bite down hard

claw—a sharp nail on the foot of an animal

dart—to move quickly from one place to another

insect—a small animal with a hard outer shell, six legs, three body sections, and two antennae; most insects have wings

mammal—a warm-blooded animal that breathes air; mammals have hair or fur; female mammals feed milk to their young

predator—an animal that hunts other animals for food

troop—a group of primates

twins—two babies born to the same mother at the same time

Read More

Kalman, Bobbie. *Baby Lemurs*. It's Fun to Learn about Baby Animals. New York: Crabtree Pub., 2011.

Monkeys. DK Readers. New York: DK Publishing, 2012.

Schreiber, Anne. *Monkeys*. New York: National Geographic Children's Books, 2013.

Internet Sites

FactHound offers a safe, fun way to find Internet sites related to this book. All of the sites on FactHound have been researched by our staff.

Here's all you do:

Visit *www.facthound.com*

Type in this code: 9781620651070

Super-cool stuff!

Check out projects, games and lots more at
www.capstonekids.com

Index

Word Count: 185
Grade: 1–2
Early-Intervention Level: 21